hollerdata

RECODE IN VBA

BY G.BLANCO

RECODE IN VBA

Published by Holler Data LLC, 382 NE 191ST ST #65220, Miami, FL 33179 USA

hollerdata.com

ISBN: 978-0-578-46652-1

TABLE OF CONTENTS

DEVELOPER TAB 1
THE VISUAL BASIC EDITOR (VBE) 2
CREATING A MODULE 3
VBA PROGRAMMING DOWN TO BASICS 4
DEFINING A MACRO 4
ABOUT VBA COMMENTS 5
SELECT METHOD 5
DECLARING VARIABLES 9
DEFINING VARIABLES 10
OBJECT VARIABLES 11
SET STATEMENT 11
USING FUNCTIONS 12
DATE FUNCTION 12
DATEADD FUNCTION 13
UNDERSTANDING VBA FLOW 15
CREATING A MACRO AND DEFINING VARIABLES 16
SELECTING AND SETTING CELL RANGE 17
CONTROLLING CODE EXECUTION 18
FOR EACH...NEXT 18
DO...LOOP 19
IF...THEN 21
HARDCODING 24
CODING THIS MACRO 25
NEW INVOICE MACRO 28
TRIGGERING MACROS 33
FORM CONTROLS 33
ACTIVEX CONTROLS 36
CALLING ALL MACROS 37
ACTIVEX CONTROL MACRO 41
FINAL NOTES 48

COMPANION FILES

ABOUT THE AUTHOR

G. BLANCO is a data-driven individual based in Miami who has previously held data-related positions at several companies including Cisco Systems, Hewlett-Packard, and Office Depot. He has a master's degree in Predictive Analytics from Northwestern University.

ABOUT THIS MINIBOOK

You'll quickly learn how to write an Excel macro in VBA, how to create variables to interact with your data. You'll also learn how to write loops to control your code execution, and how to iterate through your workbook cells. This minibook will give you the knowledge you need to quickly get started in serious VBA programming.

The goal of this minibook is to give you a full Excel macro already coded for you to re-program. The macro calculates invoice due dates depending on different conditions for a high volume of invoices. It moves around Excel to perform tasks through controlled executions. Keep in mind this minibook is not about how to calculate invoice due dates, rather, it's about giving you practical knowledge to jump-start you into VBA.

If you have already bought a book about VBA even better; this minibook will reinforce and show you how to apply that knowledge. It's packed with simple and useful statements for automation.

HOW TO CONTACT US

Please address comments and questions concerning this book to the publisher at **holler@hollerdata.com**.

HOW TO NAVIGATE THIS MINIBOOK

This minibook comes with two companion files, an Excel template and a .txt file containing all source code. **Find the download link to access the companion files at the very end of this minibook.**

DEVELOPER TAB

You'll find all the developer tools you'd need in the DEVELOPER tab.

If you don't have the DEVELOPER tab already visible, go to **FILE**, select **Options**, then select **Customize Ribbon** and under **Main Tabs** enable **Developer** as shown in Figure 1.

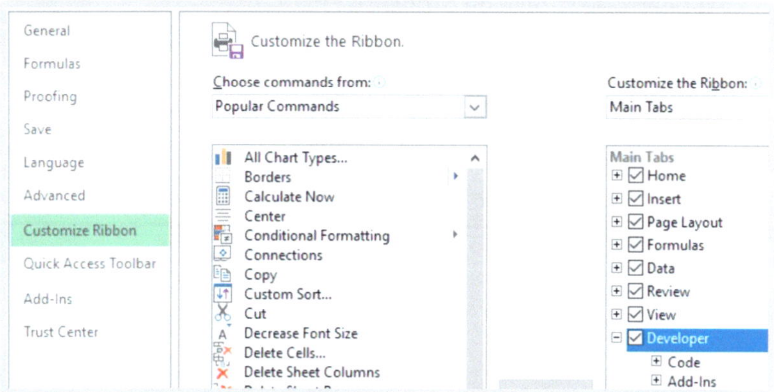

Figure 1.

Open this minibook's companion file and save it as **Excel Macro-Enabled Template**. Be warned, if you save the template in any other format your macros won't work.

THE VISUAL BASIC EDITOR (VBE)

To code in Visual Basic for Applications (VBA), you need to work in the Visual Basic Editor (VBE).

Once the Excel file is opened, to open the *Visual Basic Editor*, on the ribbon go to **DEVELOPER** and click in **Visual Basic** (located on the left side of the ribbon) as shown in Figure 2. You should see the *Visual Basic Editor* opened and its appearance should be similar to Figure 4.

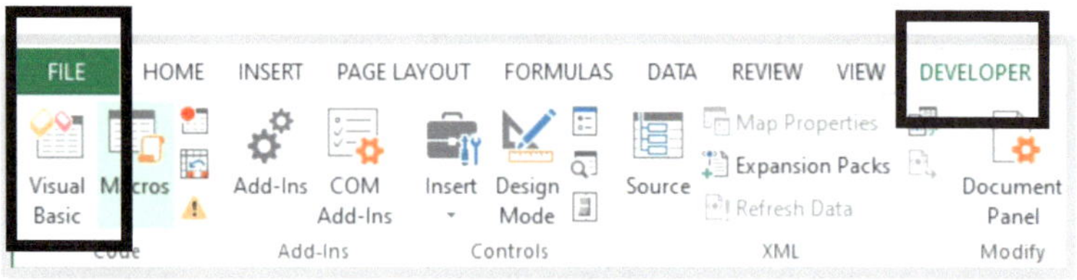

Figure 2.

CREATING A MODULE

To create a macro, start by creating a new module.

In the VBE, go to **Project Window** and do a right click anywhere below the tree diagram. Click **Insert** and select **Module** as per Figure 4. If the **Project Window** is not visible, go to **View** and click on **Project Explorer**. The newly created *Module 1* should be visible. We're all set to start writing VBA code.

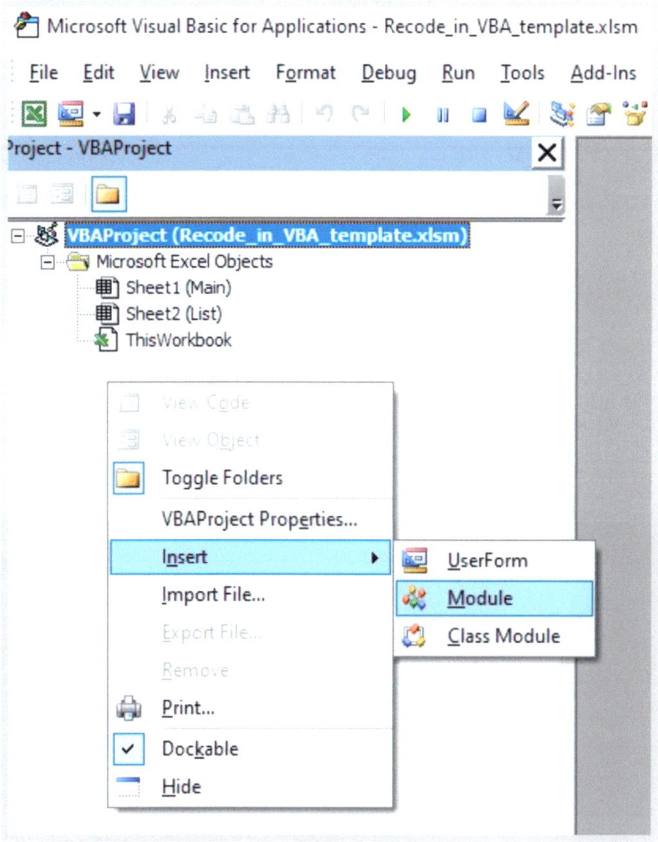

Figure 4.

VBA PROGRAMMING DOWN TO BASICS

This part of the booklet lays out some basic concepts and steps that will help you understand how to write VBA code.

If you're new to VBA, read this part so that the later sections of this minibook can be understood.

DEFINING A MACRO

Macros can be created by typing ***Sub*** followed by ***MacroName ()***. Let's create a macro called *test_macro*. Go to the *Code Window* and making sure *Module1* is highlighted. Type the following:

Sub test_macro()

Note that *End Sub* just appeared at the end. See Figure 6 for details.

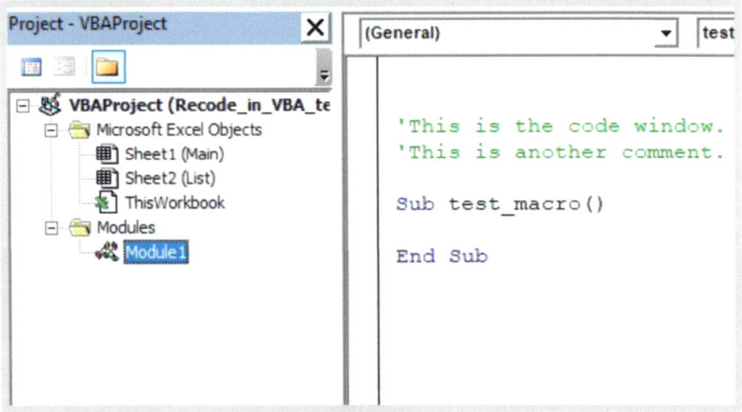

Figure 6.

HOW IT WORKS

Sub stands for sub-procedure, which makes reference to a set of instructions. Simply stated, ***Sub MacroName()*** sets where the macro begins and also gives the macro a unique identifier (its name). ***End Sub*** sets where the macro ends. All code contained in this macro needs to be written between these two lines.

ABOUT VBA COMMENTS

Documenting what your code does is considered good practice. Comments throughout your script will let you (and others) understand at a glance what a particular block of code does when it's run.

Every time you insert text into your macro with a preceding apostrophe ('), you insert a comment. VBA won't execute the comments, they'll just be there to provide information about your macro. See Figure 6 for details.

SELECT METHOD

We can make use of the ***SELECT*** method to select a specific cell in our worksheet. We can also instruct Excel to move in a given direction and select multiple cells.

Let's code this macro to select cell *G14*.

1. In VBE, under *Sub test_macro()*, type ***Range("G14").Select***

Let's execute the macro.

1. Position your pointer between *Sub test_macro()* and *End Sub* and click ***Run Macro*** (*Play icon*) or go to ***Run*** and select ***Run Macro***. See Figure 7 and Figure 8 for references.

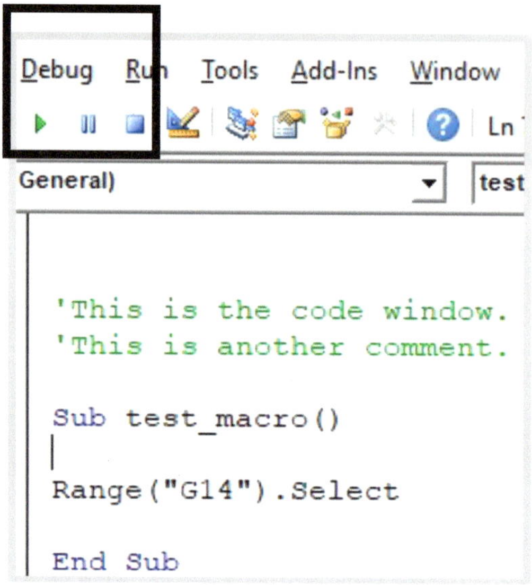

Figure 7.

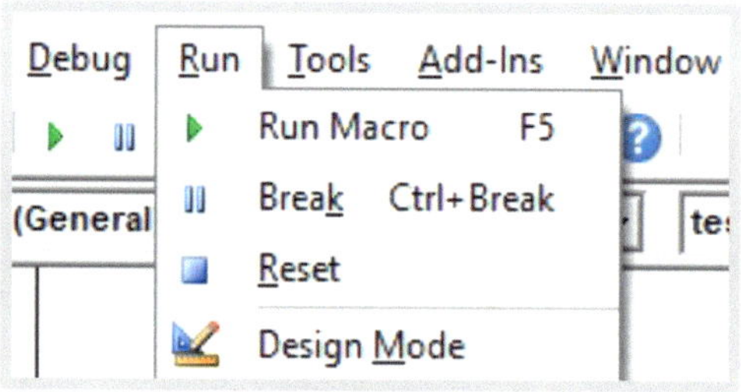

Figure 8.

Go to your worksheet and note that cell *G14* is selected. See Figure 9. Just for fun, try selecting other cells in your workbook.

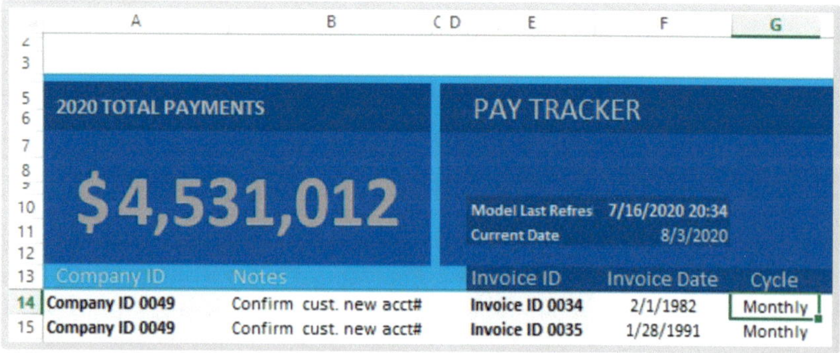

Figure 9.

Let's try something else besides selecting cell *G14*. We're going to move down to the last cell that contains data.

1. Replace previous line of code with the following: ***Range("G14").End(xlDown).Select***

Run the macro and note that this time, our modified code selected the last cell in the column. See Figures 10 and 11 for reference.

(General) | test_macro

```
'This is the code window.
'This is another comment.

Sub test_macro()

Range("G14").End(xlDown).Select

End Sub
```

Figure 10.

13	Company ID	Notes	Invoice ID	Invoice Date	Cycle
296	Company ID 0190		Invoice ID 0841	1/1/2017	Annual
297	Company ID 0190		Invoice ID 0842	5/6/1999	Quarterly
298	Company ID 0190		Invoice ID 0843	10/8/2001	Quarterly
299	Company ID 0190		Invoice ID 0844	2/3/2017	Annual
300	Company ID 0190		Invoice ID 0845	7/14/1998	Quarterly
301					
302					

Figure 11.

Let's try something else. Let's select the last cell below *G14* that contains data, and extend our selection from *G14* to that last cell.

1. Replace previous line of code with the following:

Range(Range("G14"),Range("G14").End(xlDown)).Select

See Figures 12 and 13.

(General) | test_macro

```
'This is the code window.
'This is another comment.

Sub test_macro()

Range(Range("G14"), Range("G14").End(xlDown)).Select

End Sub
```

Figure 12.

13	Company ID	Notes	Invoice ID	Invoice Date	Cycle
284	Company ID 0010		Invoice ID 0829	2/1/1990	Quarterly
285	Company ID 0010		Invoice ID 0830	3/30/1995	Quarterly
286	Company ID 0190		Invoice ID 0831	5/31/2017	Quarterly
287	Company ID 0190		Invoice ID 0832	7/1/2007	Quarterly
288	Company ID 0190		Invoice ID 0833	9/5/2017	Quarterly
289	Company ID 0190		Invoice ID 0834	3/21/2014	Quarterly
290	Company ID 0190		Invoice ID 0835	7/1/2017	Annual
291	Company ID 0190		Invoice ID 0836	7/17/1990	Annual
292	Company ID 0190		Invoice ID 0837	9/17/2003	Monthly
293	Company ID 0190		Invoice ID 0838	10/16/2000	Monthly
294	Company ID 0190	New_Invoice	Invoice ID 0839	11/4/2020	Quarterly
295	Company ID 0190		Invoice ID 0840	12/5/2001	Annual
296	Company ID 0190		Invoice ID 0841	1/1/2017	Annual
297	Company ID 0190		Invoice ID 0842	5/6/1999	Quarterly
298	Company ID 0190		Invoice ID 0843	10/8/2001	Quarterly
299	Company ID 0190		Invoice ID 0844	2/3/2017	Annual
300	Company ID 0190		Invoice ID 0845	7/14/1998	Quarterly
301					
302					

Figure 13.

HOW IT WORKS

Let's breakdown the examples to gain a better understanding of the syntax. In the first example, ***Range("G14").Select***, we used the *Range* property and the *Select* method to instruct Excel to select a *Range Object* (a cell).

In that regard, having G14 in our code by itself wouldn't mean a thing to Excel. Assigning an Object attribute to G14 (a *Range* Object attribute) through *Range()* will make G14 become a reference to a cell in our worksheet. *Range* is an object in Excel that can be represented by a single cell or multiple cells.

In the second example, ***Range("G14").End(xlDown).Select***, we added the expression *End(xlDown)* to the syntax to indicate to Excel that it should select the last cell that resides below *G14* and contains data. As well as moving down, we can also go up by using *End(xlUp)*, or to the right by using *End(xlToRight)*, or to the left by using *End(xlToLeft)*.

A thing to always consider is the syntax; we need to follow VBA's syntax to write code in the form of a statement. This implies specifying that *G14* is a *Range Object* and that the property we intend to invoke from the *Range Object* is *End(xlDown)*. This particular property in our example selects that last cell that contains data. That's what this property does. Know that properties are specific to Objects.

DECLARING VARIABLES

Variables are an important part of programming. To declare a variable we need to use the keyword ***Dim***; *Dim* stands for Dimension. The following *Dim* statement will create a variable called *Cycle* and it will declare its data type as *String*:

Dim Cycle **As** String

This other *Dim* statement will create a variable called *Current_Date* and it will declare its data type as *Date*:

Dim Current_Date **As** Date

See Figure 14 for reference.

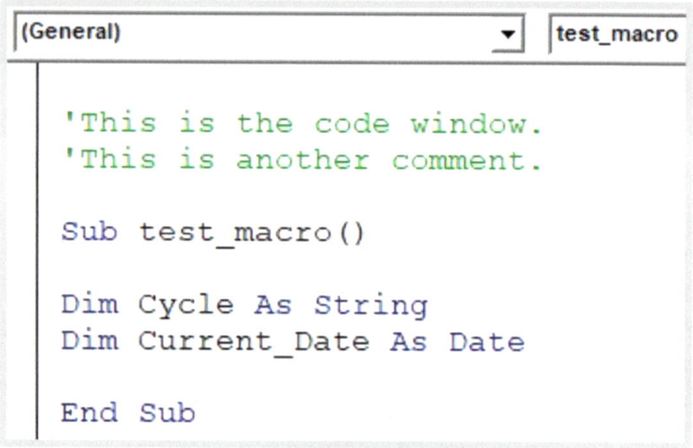

Figure 14.

TAKEAWAY

We've created two variables. Think of variables as boxes; one of them was created to store strings and the other one to store dates or even date functions. This is important, because if we needed to perform calculations involving dates, we would need variables that would allow us to perform such calculations.

DEFINING VARIABLES

After a variable exists, we can assign a value (or functions) to it. We can write statements using the equal sign (=) to store strings in string variables. The following statement assigns the expression *Annual* to variable *Cycle*. Variable *Cycle* can store the expression *Annual* since its datatype was previously declared as a sequence of characters (string). Note that *Annual* is enclosed in double quotes (strings always need to be enclosed in double quotes).

Cycle= "Annual"

TAKEAWAY

Variables provide a way to interact with your data. The word *Annual* is a discrete value that you'd find in a column of your worksheet.

OBJECT VARIABLES

Object variables represent those entities that are part of Excel. Object variables are useful for making references to objects such as worksheets, columns, rows, cells, and cell ranges.

We can use the following *Dim* statement to declare *Target_Range* as a cell range contained in our Excel worksheet:

Dim Target_Range **As Range**

TAKEAWAY

The same way we can declare a variable to contain a string or a date, we can declare a variable to contain a cell range. Later, we'll assign a cell range to *Target_Range* in order to move around Excel and perform different tasks.

SET STATEMENT

The *Set* statement is another way to assign object references to variables. I mentioned how to use the *Select* method to select an object, we previously selected cell *G14* and cell range below *G14* that contained data. With the *Set* statement, we can take that object (represented by a selection of a cell range) and assign it to a variable. See example below:

```
Range(Range("G14"), Range("G14").End(xlDown)).Select
Set Target_Range = Selection
```

HOW IT WORKS

After you execute these two statements, *Target_Range* will reference the cell range selected in the first statement. Going forward in our macro we can refer to cells *G14* to the last cell that contains data as *Target_Range*.

TAKEAWAY

These are simple and useful statements for automation. Just think about this, let's imagine you're working with financial data.As new data comes in every day, you'd want your model to be fully capable of dealing with the growing volume of data in an automated fashion.

USING FUNCTIONS

VBA provides developers with a variety of built-in functions. Built-in VBA functions can go from financial functions to file management functions. For our macro we're going to use some date functions.

DATE FUNCTION

The **Date** *function* returns the current system date. Some steps back, we declared variable *Current_Date* as *Date datatype* to enable the variable to store dates. Now, the second step will be to assign the **Date** *function* to *Current_Date* in order for *Current_Date* to return the current system date. Like this:

```
Current_Date = Date
```

Every time the macro runs, *Current_Date* will store the current system date. This is important, because in order for our macro to work, it will need to know what day is today.

TAKEAWAY

Be careful not to mix the ***Date*** *function* with the ***Date*** *datatype*. We use the word ***As*** to declare a variable's *datatype* and the = *operator* to assign a value or *function* to a *variable*. These are two different things named the same.

DATEADD FUNCTION

The ***DateAdd*** *function* in Excel provides a convenient way to add or subtract dates. Each function in Excel has its own set of arguments that we need to input in order for the function to work. For the *DateAdd* function there are three arguments to consider:

The interval argument: A string representing the time interval you intend to add or subtract. In the following examples, I only mention two types of *interval arguments*: *day* represented by ***d*** and *month* represented by ***m***. But ,there are more to choose from, for example***, yyyy*** represents *year* and ***h*** represents ***hour***.

Number: This is the number of intervals you intend to add. If you choose *day* as the interval argument, ***Number*** will represent the number of days you want the function to add.

Date Value*:* This is the date to which the interval is to be added.

To be clear, if you choose to work with ***d*** as *interval argument*, whatever ***Number*** you set in the function will be the number of days the macro is going to add to the date represented by ***Date Value***. Here is an example:

The following statement adds one day to January 25, where ***d*** is the *interval argument*, **1** represents ***Number,*** and 25-Jan-20 represents ***Date Value***. The returned value will be 26-Jan-20.

DateAdd("d", 1, "25-Jan-20")

UNDERSTANDING VBA FLOW

This section will outline some basic concepts and explain how those concepts work in a block of code.

We're going to take the macro shown below and break it apart, piece by piece, to gain a better understanding of it. This macro iterates through your worksheet's cells to perform tasks. The goal of the macro is to calculate an invoice due date given its *Cycle* and *Term* sitting in columns *G* and *I* respectively. Here's the complete macro we're going to evaluate:

```
Sub Annual_example_macro()

    Dim MyCell As Range
    Dim MyRange As Range
    Dim Payment_cycle As String
    Dim Term_1 As String
    Dim CurrentDate As Date

    Payment_cycle = "Annual"
    Term_1 = "15 days"
    CurrentDate = Date

    Range(Range("H14"), Range("H14").End(xlDown)).Select
    Set MyRange = Selection

            For Each MyCell In MyRange
                MyCell.Offset(0, -1).Select
                If Selection.Value = Payment_cycle Then
            Do
                MyCell.Value = DateAdd("m", 12, MyCell.Value)
            Loop Until CDate(MyCell.Value) >= CurrentDate
                End If
            Next MyCell

            'procedure - Term_1
            For Each MyCell In MyRange
                MyCell.Offset(0, -1).Select
                If Selection.Value = Payment_cycle Then
                MyCell.Offset(0, 1).Select
                If Selection.Value = Term_1 Then
                MyCell.Value = DateAdd("m", -12, MyCell.Value)
                MyCell.Value = DateAdd("d", 15, MyCell.Value)
                If MyCell.Value < CurrentDate Then
                MyCell.Value = DateAdd("m", 12, MyCell.Value)
                End If
                End If
                End If
            Next MyCell

End Sub
```

CREATING A MACRO AND DEFINING VARIABLES

The first step will be to define the macro by assigning a unique name to it. Next, we proceed to declare and define our variables.

```
Sub Annual_example_macro()
    'declare variables
    Dim MyCell As Range
    Dim MyRange As Range
    Dim Payment_cycle As String
    Dim Term_1 As String
    Dim CurrentDate As Date
    'define variables
    Payment_cycle = "Annual"
    Term_1 = "15 days"
    CurrentDate = Date
```

HOW IT WORKS

First, we create and define our variables:

Sub Annual_example_macro(): We created a new macro called *Annual_example_macro*.

Dim MyCell As Range: We declared variable *MyCell* as *Range*.

Dim MyRange As Range: We declared variable *MyRange* as *Range*.

Dim Payment_cycle As String: We declared variable *Payment_cycle* as *String*.

Dim Term_1 As String: We declared variable *Term_1* as String.

Dim CurrentDate As Date: We declared variable *CurrentDate* as *Date* (*datatype*).

Payment_cycle = "Annual": The string *Annual* is assigned to variable *Payment_cycle*. You'll find this same exact string in column G.

CurrentDate = Date: The *Date function* is the current system date assigned to variable *CurrentDate*. Previously defined as *Date datatype* to enable the variable to store what the *Date function* returns (a date). Variable *CurrentDate* lets the macro know what the date is today which is needed to calculate the invoice due date.

SELECTING AND SETTING CELL RANGE

In this segment, we first select a cell range, then we create a variable out of the selected cells. This variable (*MyRange*) is one of the elements that will allow us to move from cell to cell to evaluate the contents of those cells and take action depending on what's found, as you will see in the next segments.

```
Range(Range("H14"), Range("H14").End(xlDown)).Select
Set MyRange = Selection
```

HOW IT WORKS

Range(Range("H14"),Range("H14").End(xlDown)).Select: To select cell *H14* and every cell below *H14* that contains data.

Set MyRange = Selection: To state that *MyRange* equals (contains) all cells that were selected in the previous statement.

TAKEAWAY

As already mentioned, every time the macro runs these two statements will run, meaning that if your data grows, the macro's selection will expand as you add more data to your model.

CONTROLLING CODE EXECUTION

Iterate through your cells and enable decision making capabilities.

FOR EACH...NEXT

In the previous step, we created a variable called *MyRange* which is a selection of a cell range. You can use VBA's ***For Each...Next Statement*** to iterate through cells that are contained in *MyRange*. Like this:

```
For Each MyCell In MyRange
    MyCell.Offset(0, -1).Select
    If Selection.Value = Payment_cycle Then
Do
    MyCell.Value = DateAdd("m", 12, MyCell.Value)
Loop Until CDate(MyCell.Value) >= CurrentDate
    End If
Next MyCell
```

Note, the syntax for *For Each...Next Statement* is as follows:

For Each *element* ***In*** *group*
Statements...
Next *element*

HOW IT WORKS

Where the element is an element of the group. In this case the element (*MyCell*) is each cell of the group, and the group is the cell range contained in variable *MyRange*.

What this does is tell Excel that for each cell in *MyRange* you want to perform one or more actions. Excel will step on the first cell of the group (cell *H14*), perform one or more actions, and then move to the next cell (instructed by *Next MyCell*) to perform the same set of actions. Next, how that works in more detail.

DO...LOOP

You can make use of ***Do*** to repeat a group of *statements* until a certain *condition* becomes true. VBA provides more than one way to run the *Do...Loop statement*. You can use *Loop Until* to keep running whatever line of code you need to run until certain *condition* is satisfied.

What this *Do...Loop* does is to bring the date that will be sitting in cell *H14* to the current year, along with the rest of the dates also sitting in column *H*. At the time this macro runs, the date sitting in column *H* will be the same *Invoice Date* sitting in column *F*.

HOW IT WORKS

For Each MyCell In MyRange : Tell Excel to iterate through the elements of the collection, that is, step into each cell contained in *MyRange* and take the following actions:

MyCell.Offset(0, -1).Select: After selecting the first cell of *MyRange* (*H14*), this line of code instructs Excel to move to the left one cell (instructed by Offset(0,-1)) and select that cell (*G14*).

If Selection.Value = Payment_cycle Then: If the selected cell (*G14*) is equal to Payment_cycle (*Annual*) do the following:

Do: To open (execute) a Do...Loop.

MyCell.Value = DateAdd("m", 12, MyCell.Value): Add 12 months to the date contained in cell *H14*.

Loop Until CDate(MyCell.Value) >= CurrentDate: Keep adding 12 months until the date contained in cell *H14* is greater than or equal to the current system date. In other words, keep adding 12 months until the condition *H14 >= CurrentDate* becomes True.

End If: Close the *If statement* previously opened, every single *If* statement needs to be closed with an *End If* statement.

Next MyCell: Make Excel jump to the next cell contained in *MyRange*, that is, cell *H15*, and perform the same exact steps that were performed in cell *H14*. After cell *H15* is done, the macro will move to the next cell (*H16*), and will keep looping until it reaches the last cell contained in *MyRange*.

Just so you know, before this macro runs another macro will copy and paste all dates from column *F* (*Invoice Date*) into column *H* (*Due Date*). This step is convenient, because every time this macro runs it starts calculating the invoice's due-date in column *H* from the invoice's start date, thus refreshing all previously calculated due-dates that are (will be) sitting in column *H*.

The point is, in this segment the macro moves from cell to cell using the *Do...Loop* to add 12 months until a certain condition becomes true. In this case, the condition is that the date sitting in cell *H14* is greater (when working with dates greater means after) or equal to *CurrentDate*.

For instance, if you have an invoice from 2018 and we're in the year 2025, the macro will add 12 months to 2018 until the year 2025 is reached, which should be the system date at the time. The following statements that are part of the next piece of code will take the resultant date and finish calculating every invoice due-date that is paid annually with a payment term of 15 days.

IF...THEN

You can also control your code execution using ***If...Then Statements*** to execute certain actions depending on the value contained in a given cell of the selected range (*MyRange*). Keep in mind that the ***If...Then Statement*** provides Excel with decision making capability.

Bottom line, ***For Each...Next Statement*** will let you move through all cells contained in MyRange and ***If...Then Statement*** will let you decide what to do when, for example, the string *Annual* is found.

```
For Each MyCell In MyRange
    MyCell.Offset(0, -1).Select
    If Selection.Value = Payment_cycle Then
    MyCell.Offset(0, 1).Select
    If Selection.Value = Term_1 Then
    MyCell.Value = DateAdd("m", -12, MyCell.Value)
    MyCell.Value = DateAdd("d", 15, MyCell.Value)
    If MyCell.Value < CurrentDate Then
    MyCell.Value = DateAdd("m", 12, MyCell.Value)
    End If
    End If
    End If
Next MyCell
End Sub
```

HOW IT WORKS

Let's evaluate this block of code line by line. The ***For Each...Next Statement*** is created (**For Each** at the beginning of the block and ***Next*** at the end):

For Each MyCell In MyRange : Here, we instruct Excel to iterate through the elements of the collection. That is, step into each cell contained in *MyRange* and take the following actions:

MyCell.Offset(0, -1).Select: This line of code will move to the left (instructed by Offset(0,-1)) from *MyRange* (*H14*) and Select cell *G14*.

If Selection.Value = Payment_cycle Then: If the selected cell (*G14*) is equal to *Payment_cycle* (we declared *Payment_cycle* as a String and assigned the value *Annu*al to it) do the following:

MyCell.Offset(0, 1).Select: Here we stand again in *MyCell* which in this case is *H14* and by executing *Offset(0,1)* Excel moves one cell to the right (to cell *I14*). Note that we use *Offset(0,-1)* to move one cell to the left and *Offset(0,1)* to move one cell to the right.

If Selection.Value = Term_1 Then: If the selected cell value (*I14*) equals *Term_1* (*15 days*), then do the following:

MyCell.Value = DateAdd("m", -12, MyCell.Value): This line of code triggers a *DateAdd* function where Excel subtracts 12 months from whatever date is in cell *H14* (as mentioned before, at this point this is *Invoice Date*).

MyCell.Value = DateAdd("d", 15, MyCell.Value): Excel adds 15 days to the date that resulted from prior step subtraction.

If MyCell.Value < CurrentDate Then: Here is another step where decision making happens, if the date contained in *H14* (that resulted from prior steps subtraction and addition) is less (less means before when we're dealing with dates) than *CurrentDate* (current system date) then do the following:

MyCell.Value = DateAdd("m", 12, MyCell.Value): Add 12 months to the date contained in *H14*.

End If: Every time you open an ***If...Then Statement*** you need to close the statement with an ***End If***, always. In this case, we opened three If's and therefore we need three End If's.

Next MyCell: Excel jumps to the next cell contained in *MyRange* (*H15*) and performs, once again, the same set of actions. After *H15* is done, Excel will move to the next cell in *MyRange*, which is *H16*. After there are no more cells to move to, the macro will stop.

End Sub: This is always the last statement to end the macro.

You may be wondering why we subtracted 12 months to later add 15 days and finally add 12 months. We first subtract 12 months and added 15 days to find out if we are still running under the last TERM. If the current date is greater (greater means after when dealing with dates) than the due-date calculated by the step, that means last payment term is over and the macro will give you the next due-date.

This makes more sense when you are calculating monthly due-dates. For example, you have a new monthly invoice that starts in January with a 60 day payment term. That means that after January 31 you still have 60 days to pay the invoice.

Suppose you are in February. If you are running the model in February you need to make sure that the tool shows you the remaining days left to pay the invoice in the month of January instead of calculating the due-date for February. That's why we add and then subtract dates to add again. When the invoice from January is past-due in March, the macro will calculate the next invoice due-date; that is, the due-date from the month of February.

HARDCODING

Hardcoding in programming means fixing some or all of your program's parameters using actual data values. Hence, hardcoding may reduce the flexibility of your code. The only way to modify any hardcoded parameter is by going into your code and manually changing the parameter itself.

People often argue that hardcoding is bad practice and it should be avoided when possible. I don't see it that way, as long as a limited number of parameters are hardcoded. If you can avoid it, go ahead and do so, but if not, it doesn't mean you are compromising your program's flexibility or that it can be written in a better way.

For instance, cell *H14* is hardcoded into the macro. This is column *Due Date* which is the macro's pointer column/cell. The macro moves from cell to cell starting from cell *H14*. You can use any other cell as a starting point to iterate through your columns/cells. You do so by simply manually changing in your source code cell *H14* to any other cell.

```
Range(Range("H14"), Range("H14").End(xlDown)).Select
Set MyRange = Selection
```

Something to have in mind, *CurrentDate* is not hardcoded since it does not take any specific fixed date; instead its value depends on a function which supplies the current system date. Meaning that its value changes without the need to modify the source code.

```
CurrentDate = Date
```

```
Loop Until CDate(MyCell.Value) >= CurrentDate
```

CODING THIS MACRO

In this section, everything comes together in a simple way, giving particular attention to details.

In this chapter, you're going to write VBA procedures using the code and dummy data I provided. You also have the option to copy and paste the source code into the VBE.

Be careful when coding; any punctuation mark missing or out of place, any misspelled word, etc. will generate an error and will stop you from running your macro successfully. Usually, programmers spend hours trying to fix errors, and that's because it's often hard to find them.

Delete all code from *MODULE 1* (if any) and write or paste the source code provided.

Here are some key points to consider when writing macros to calculate payment due-dates based on monthly cycles:

- Assign string *Monthly* to variable *Payment_cycle*. By doing this, the macro will be able to identify which invoices are marked as monthly in column *G* of your spreadsheet. Don't forget to add quotation marks.
- Make sure to adjust your *DateAdd* functions to whatever your payment cycle is. Since this macro calculates monthly cycles, we're using *m* as interval to make sure one month is added every time the function runs.
- Set up all your different payment terms. Assign strings of text *15 days, 30 days* and *60 days* to variables *Term_1*, *Term_2* and *Term_3* respectively. This way the macro will be able to identify the correct *Term* from column *I* for each invoice. Remember to add quotation marks.

- Create a macro with a unique name. In this script, the macro's name is *Monthly_calculation_macro*. This is hardcoded into the *Trigger* macro. (More details about the *Trigger* macro in the following sections).

In *Module 1*, write the block of code below, or copy and paste it from the source-code file.

'Step One – Name your macro:

```
Sub Monthly_calculation_macro()
```

'Step Two – Declare your variables:

```
Dim MyCell As Range
Dim MyRange As Range
Dim Payment_cycle As String
Dim Term_1 As String
Dim Term_2 As String
Dim Term_3 As String
Dim CurrentDate As Date
```

'Step Three – Define your variables:

```
Payment_cycle = "Monthly"
Term_1 = "15 days"
Term_2 = "30 days"
Term_3 = "60 days"
CurrentDate = Date
```

'Step Four – Write instructions as follows:

'First block of instructions: This block assigns a cell range to *MyRange* and calculates the 'ready date'.

```
Range(Range("H14"), Range("H14").End(xlDown)).Select
Set MyRange = Selection

        For Each MyCell In MyRange
            MyCell.Offset(0, -1).Select
            If Selection.Value = Payment_cycle Then
        Do
            MyCell.Value = DateAdd("m", 1, MyCell.Value)
        Loop Until CDate(MyCell.Value) >= CurrentDate
            End If
        Next MyCell
```

'Second block of instructions: This block calculates due-dates for the first Term.

```
For Each MyCell In MyRange
    MyCell.Offset(0, -1).Select
    If Selection.Value = Payment_cycle Then
    MyCell.Offset(0, 1).Select
    If Selection.Value = Term_1 Then
    MyCell.Value = DateAdd("m", -1, MyCell.Value)
    MyCell.Value = DateAdd("d", 15, MyCell.Value)
    If MyCell.Value < CurrentDate Then
    MyCell.Value = DateAdd("m", 1, MyCell.Value)
    End If
    End If
    End If
Next MyCell
```

'Third block of instructions: This block calculates due-dates for the second Term.

```
For Each MyCell In MyRange
    MyCell.Offset(0, -1).Select
    If Selection.Value = Payment_cycle Then
    MyCell.Offset(0, 1).Select
    If Selection.Value = Term_2 Then
    MyCell.Value = DateAdd("m", -1, MyCell.Value)
    MyCell.Value = DateAdd("d", 30, MyCell.Value)
    If MyCell.Value < CurrentDate Then
    MyCell.Value = DateAdd("m", 1, MyCell.Value)
    End If
    End If
    End If
Next MyCell
```

'Fourth block of instructions: This block calculates due-dates for the third Term.

```
For Each MyCell In MyRange
    MyCell.Offset(0, -1).Select
    If Selection.Value = Payment_cycle Then
    MyCell.Offset(0, 1).Select
    If Selection.Value = Term_3 Then
    MyCell.Value = DateAdd("m", -1, MyCell.Value)
    MyCell.Value = DateAdd("d", 60, MyCell.Value)
    If MyCell.Value < CurrentDate Then
    MyCell.Value = DateAdd("m", 1, MyCell.Value)
    End If
    End If
    End If
Next MyCell
```

'Step Five – End the macro:

```
End Sub
```

TAKEAWAY

You'll notice that *Payment_cycle, Term*, and *DateAdd* function parameters are the only variables that change with respect to the other macros (annual and quarterly macros). Everything else stays the same.

NEW INVOICE MACRO

The previous macro calculates invoice due-dates, making sure that the payment term for the last month, quarter, or year isn't over yet before giving us the next due-date. For new invoices, it's different. We don't need to take into consideration previous payment terms because there aren't any; the invoice is new and we need to calculate the date for the first payment only.

In that way, the *New Invoice* macro that we're going to write next doesn't have to go back to verify whether or not the current term is over, making it much simpler. Given that, we're going to take this opportunity to mix things up a little, and instead of writing one macro per each cycle, we're going to consolidate the code and write one macro for all cycles.

In the future, you'll realize that these series of macros can be consolidated into one, but for the sake of simplicity, I decided to split the macro into a series of smaller blocks (monthly, quarterly, and annual macros) so the code can be better understood and modified more easily.

As a note, every time the macro finds a new invoice (an invoice which starts on a date ahead of the current date) it will write *New_Invoice* in column *B* (*Notes*).

'Step One – Name your macro:

```
Sub new_invoice()
```

'Step Two – Declare your variables:

```
Dim MyCell As Range
Dim MyRange As Range
Dim Payment_cycle As String
Dim Term_1 As String
Dim Term_2 As String
Dim Term_3 As String
Dim CurrentDate As Date
Dim NewInvoice As Date
```

'Step Three – Define your variables:

```
Payment_cycle_M = "Monthly"
Payment_cycle_Q = "Quarterly"
Payment_cycle_A = "Annual"
Term_1 = "15 days"
Term_2 = "30 days"
Term_3 = "60 days"
CurrentDate = Date
```

'Step Four – Write instructions as follows:

'First block of instructions: This block defines MyRange and calculates due-dates for monthly 'invoices under all Terms.

```
Range(Range("F14"), Range("F14").End(xlDown)).Select
Set MyRange = Selection

'Monthly Cycle
For Each MyCell In MyRange
    MyCell.Offset(0, 1).Select
    If Selection.Value = Payment_cycle_M Then
    NewInvoice = DateAdd("m", 1, MyCell.Value)
    If NewInvoice >= CurrentDate Then
    MyCell.Offset(0, 3).Select

    If Selection.Value = Term_1 Then
    MyCell.Offset(0, 2).Select
    Selection.Value = DateAdd("m", 1, MyCell.Value) + 15
    MyCell.Offset(0, -4).Select
    Selection.Value = "New_Invoice"

    ElseIf Selection.Value = Term_2 Then
    MyCell.Offset(0, 2).Select
    Selection.Value = DateAdd("m", 1, MyCell.Value) + 30
    MyCell.Offset(0, -4).Select
    Selection.Value = "New_Invoice"

    Else:
    Selection.Value = Term_3
    MyCell.Offset(0, 2).Select
    Selection.Value = DateAdd("m", 1, MyCell.Value) + 60
    MyCell.Offset(0, -4).Select
    Selection.Value = "New_Invoice"
    End If
    End If
    End If
Next MyCell
```

'Second block of instructions: This block calculates due-dates for quarterly invoices under all 'Terms.

```
'Quarterly Cycle
For Each MyCell In MyRange
    MyCell.Offset(0, 1).Select
    If Selection.Value = Payment_cycle_Q Then
    NewInvoice = DateAdd("q", 1, MyCell.Value)
    If NewInvoice >= CurrentDate Then
    MyCell.Offset(0, 3).Select

    If Selection.Value = Term_1 Then
    MyCell.Offset(0, 2).Select
    Selection.Value = DateAdd("q", 1, MyCell.Value) + 15
    MyCell.Offset(0, -4).Select
    Selection.Value = "New_Invoice"

    ElseIf Selection.Value = Term_2 Then
    MyCell.Offset(0, 2).Select
    Selection.Value = DateAdd("q", 1, MyCell.Value) + 30
    MyCell.Offset(0, -4).Select
    Selection.Value = "New_Invoice"

    Else:
    Selection.Value = Term_3
    MyCell.Offset(0, 2).Select
    Selection.Value = DateAdd("q", 1, MyCell.Value) + 60
    MyCell.Offset(0, -4).Select
    Selection.Value = "New_Invoice"
    End If
    End If
    End If
Next MyCell
```

'Third block of instructions: This block calculates due-dates for annual invoices under all Terms.

```
'Annual Cycle
For Each MyCell In MyRange
    MyCell.Offset(0, 1).Select
    If Selection.Value = Payment_cycle_A Then
    NewInvoice = DateAdd("m", 12, MyCell.Value)
    If NewInvoice >= CurrentDate Then
    MyCell.Offset(0, 3).Select

    If Selection.Value = Term_1 Then
    MyCell.Offset(0, 2).Select
    Selection.Value = DateAdd("m", 12, MyCell.Value) + 15
    MyCell.Offset(0, -4).Select
    Selection.Value = "New_Invoice"

    ElseIf Selection.Value = Term_2 Then
    MyCell.Offset(0, 2).Select
    Selection.Value = DateAdd("m", 12, MyCell.Value) + 30
    MyCell.Offset(0, -4).Select
    Selection.Value = "New_Invoice"

    Else:
    Selection.Value = Term_3
    MyCell.Offset(0, 2).Select
    Selection.Value = DateAdd("m", 12, MyCell.Value) + 60
    MyCell.Offset(0, -4).Select
    Selection.Value = "New_Invoice"
    End If
    End If
    End If
Next MyCell
```

'Step Five – End the macro:

```
End Sub
```

TRIGGERING MACROS

A simple way to call all your macros.

FORM CONTROLS

Let's create a *Form Control* from where we can run all the macros at once. Go to the DEVELOPER tab and click **Insert** icon, then under **Form Controls** select **Button**. Figure 15 shows where the Button is located.

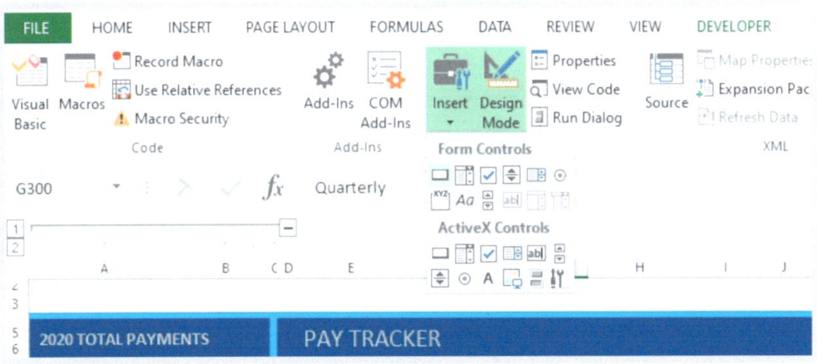

Figure 15.

Now, click somewhere on cell E7 to start drawing your Button. While pressing your mouse left button, move to somewhere around cell I8. I say somewhere around because you can make this button as big or as small as you like; it's up to you. Just make sure **Design Mode** is selected (located next to the Insert icon). Every time you need to format or adjust one of your controls, **Design Mode** needs to be activated. Remembering this will save you a lot of trouble.

Right after you draw your Button, Excel is going to ask if you would like to assign a macro. Click **Cancel,** we're going to assign a macro later. See Figure 16 and Figure 17.

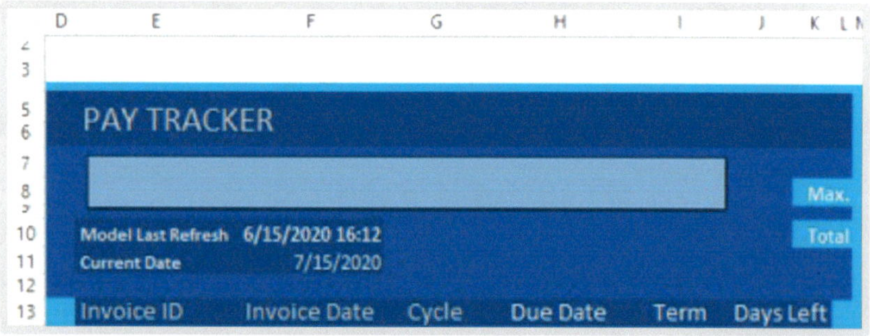

Figure 16.

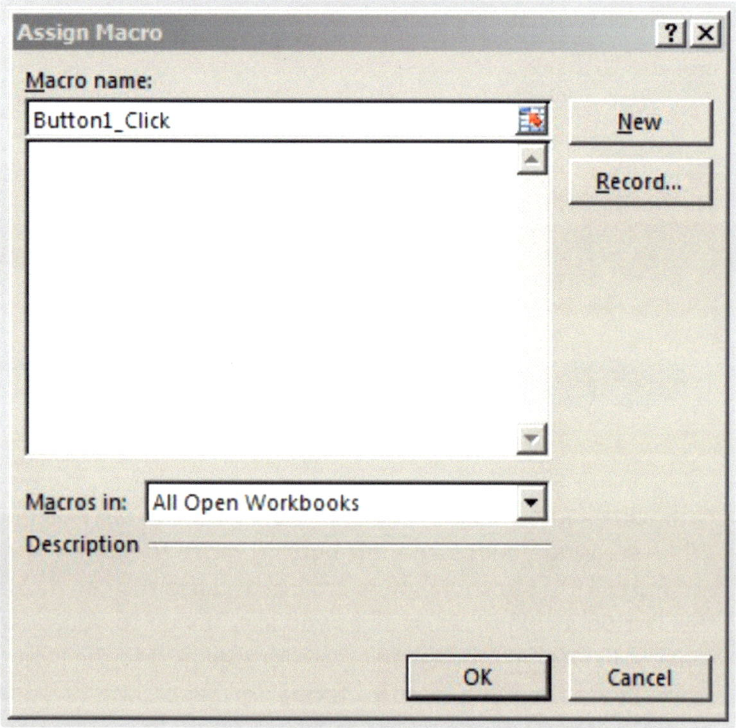

Figure 17.

Position your mouse pointer on top of the Button you just created, do a right click, and select **Edit Text** as per Figure 18.

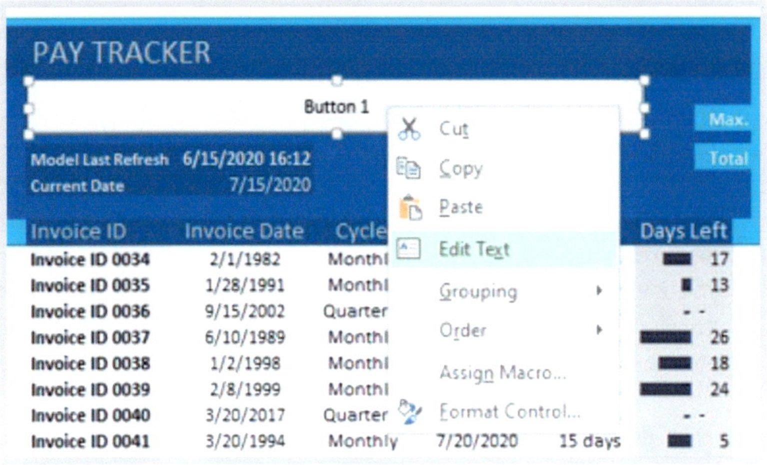

Figure 18.

This procedure gives you the option to rewrite the text that appears on the Button itself. Delete text *Button 1* and rewrite to something similar to REFRESH. See Figure 19.

Figure 19.

ACTIVEX CONTROLS

Let's create a *Combo Box* control; this type of *ActiveX* control is generally known as drop-down.

To create an *ActiveX* control, go to the Ribbon and click on the DEVELOPER tab. Make sure **Design Mode** is selected, click **Insert** and under **ActiveX Controls** click **Combo Box** as per Figure 20. After making the selection, click somewhere near cell G9 and while holding your mouse left button move to somewhere around cell I9 as shown in Figure 21. Release your mouse left button and what you've created should look similar to Figure 22. You can press the *ESC* key to deselect your *ActiveX* control.

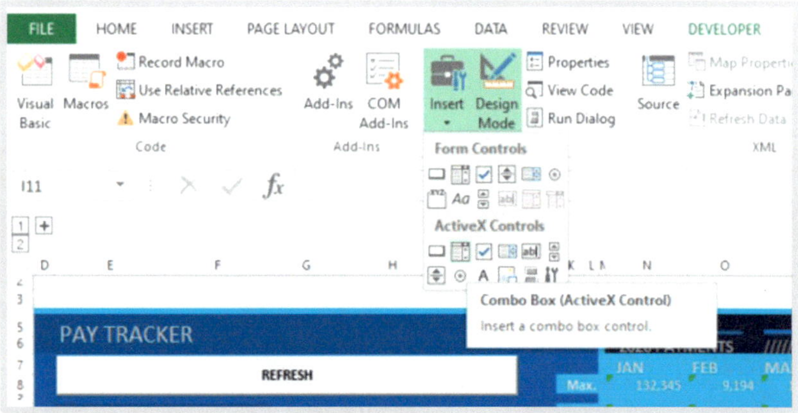

Figure 20.

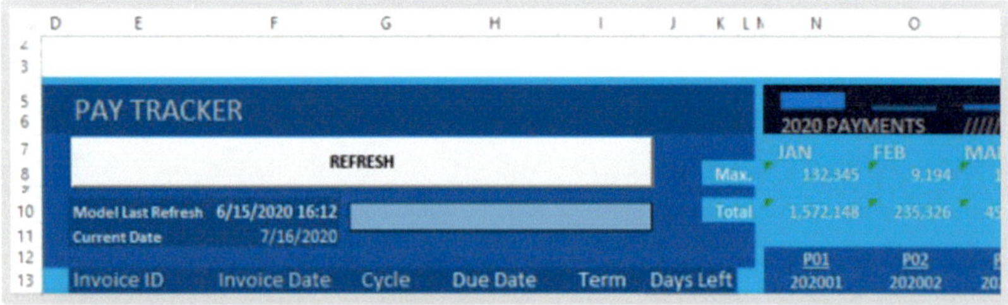

Figure 21.

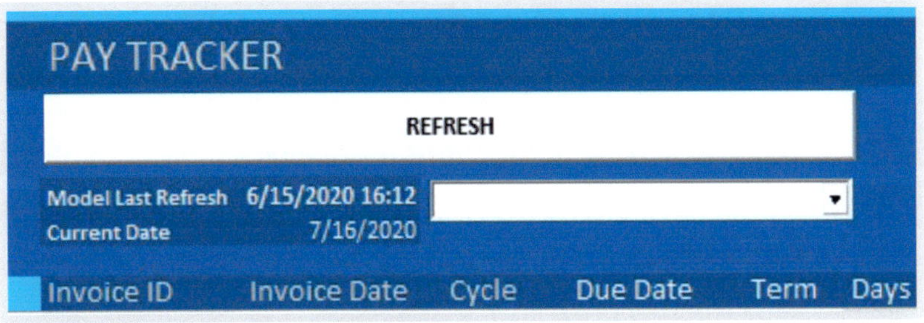

Figure 22.

We're done here. So far, we've created many of the elements your application needs to run nicely. Also, we've given some aesthetic touches to our model.

CALLING ALL MACROS

We've created several macros. It is relatively easy to put all these macros to work sequentially. We need to write a macro to call all macros. Using the *Call* statement to trigger every one of our macros is one way to do the trick.

We're going to use the *Form Control* that we just embedded in the main tab of our spreadsheet to call all procedures with just a click of a button.

Before calling all procedures, this *trigger* macro also copies and pastes dates from column *F* (*Invoice Date*) to column *H* (*Due Date*). The reason behind this step, as mentioned before, is to have a starting point from which to compute due-dates. In other words, every time the macro runs, the starting date of an invoice is copied and pasted into column *Due Date* for our macros to start calculating the invoice due-date based on the invoice's starting date.

Write the block of code below or copy and paste it from the source-code file as shown in Figure 23:

'Step One – Name your macro:

```
Sub refresh_tracker_Button_Click()
```

'Step Two – Write instructions as follows:

'First block of instructions: This block copies all dates from column F to H.

```
Range("F14").Select
Range(Selection, Selection.End(xlDown)).Select
Selection.Copy
Range("H14").Select
Selection.PasteSpecial Paste:=xlPasteValues, _
Operation:=xlNone, SkipBlanks:=False, Transpose:=False
Application.CutCopyMode = False
Range("H14").Select
```

'Second block of instructions: This block calls all macros we have written.

```
Call Montly_calculation_macro
Call Annual_calculation_macro
Call Quarter_calculation_macro
Call new_invoice
```

'Third block of instructions: This block populates the current date in cell F10 (to keep a record of the last time the model was run), then selects cell E8.

```
Range("F10") = Now
Range("F8").Select
```

'Step Three – End the macro:

```
End Sub
```

Note: Before running this macro you need to write all macros we are calling in the second block.

(General) | refresh_tracker_Button_Click

```
'*********************************************
'        T R I G G E R   M A C R O          *
'*********************************************


Sub refresh_tracker_Button_Click()

    Range("F14").Select
    Range(Selection, Selection.End(xlDown)).Select
    Selection.Copy
    Range("H14").Select
    Selection.PasteSpecial Paste:=xlPasteValues, _
    Operation:=xlNone, SkipBlanks:=False, Transpose:=False
    Application.CutCopyMode = False
    Range("H14").Select

'call macros to calculate due date
Call Montly_calculation_macro
Call Annual_calculation_macro
Call Quarter_calculation_macro
Call new_invoice

    Range("F10") = Now
    Range("F8").Select

End Sub
```

Figure 23.

Next, you need to assign *refresh_tracker_Button_Click* macro to the *Buttom Form Control* embedded in the model's main tab. Here's how:

Step One – Go to your main tab and right click on top of the Button Form Control:

Click on Assign Macro... as per figure below. **Figure 24.**

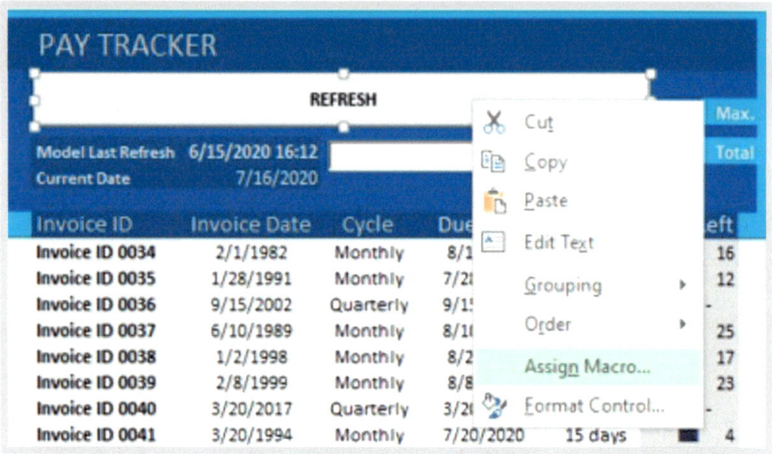

Figure 24.

Step Two – Assign macro:

Click on *refresh_tracker_Button_Click* and click *OK* as per Figure 25.

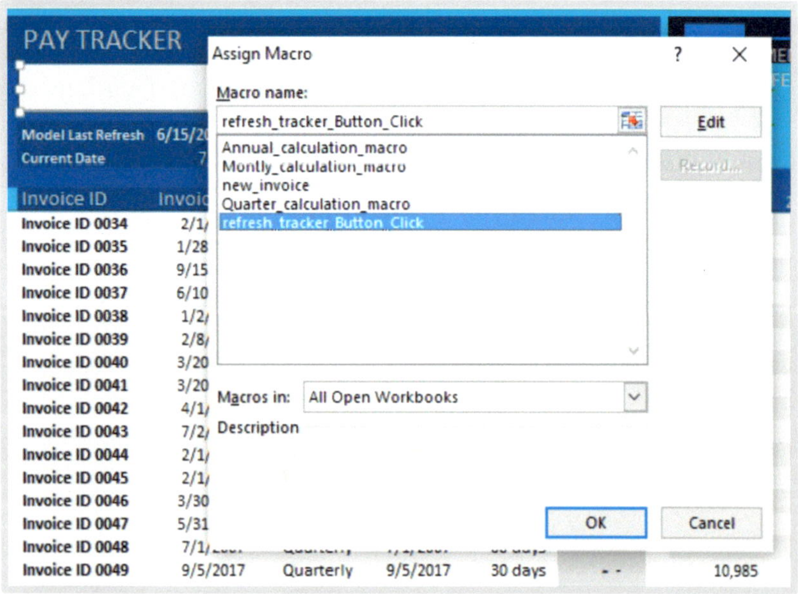

Figure 25.

Clicking *REFRESH SCHEDULER* will activate your trigger macro which calls all macros we coded. Note, in this case we're assigning to the *Button Form Control* a macro that calls multiple macros but you can simply add any macro you want to the *Button* or create more buttons to call macros individually.

ACTIVEX CONTROL MACRO

A few steps back, we created an *ActiveX Control*, and now we're going to assign a macro to it. The goal of the control (list dropdown) is to filter one or more invoices previously grouped by *Company ID* (column *A*).

To illustrate with an example see Figure 26. Note that all of the invoices belong to *Company ID 0049*. Assigning invoices to parent companies (those entities which issued the invoice) should be done when they're entered into the model. The dummy data was fabricated to group companies using an identifier such as *Company ID* but as you can imagine, you can actually set a name of a specific group or person here (or whatever name or grouping code works best for you); or you can leave it blank if no grouping is needed.

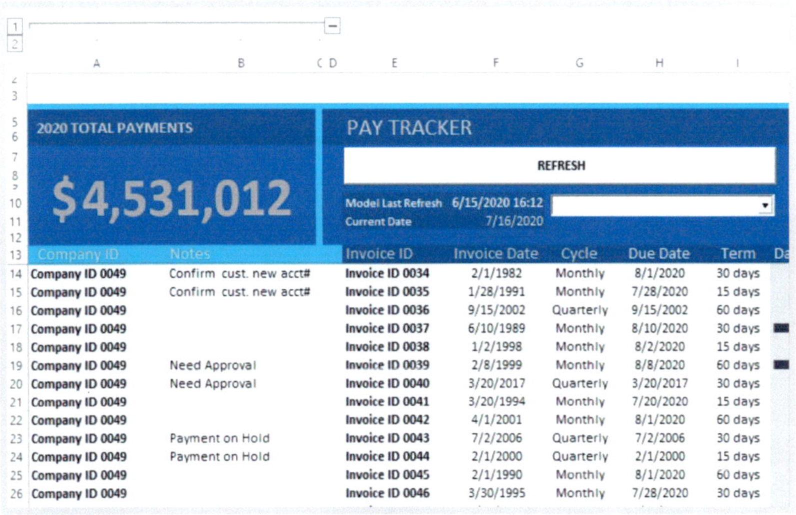

Figure 26.

To keep working on our *ActiveX Control*, we're going to create a list of groupings. To do so, we need to create a new sheet and name it *List*. Just click the plus icon (+) next to *Main* sheet to create the new sheet. Note, this step is not needed since the *List* sheet is already created.

After the new sheet is created, we need to give it a name. Right-click on the new *Sheet* tab and click **Rename** to set a name as we did before. See Figure 27. Note, since we're going to hardcode the name of this sheet in our macro, it's better if we stick to the name for the macro to work. In other words, if we change the name of this sheet in the future, we need to modify the macro (that we're going to write next) to replace the old sheet's name with the new one.

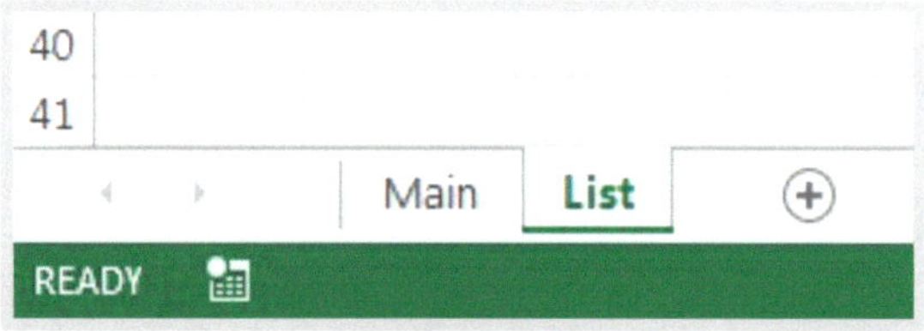

Figure 27.

With the *List* sheet in place, we can proceed to establish a list of names to place in our drop down's source list. Every time a new name or entity is added to column A (*Company ID*), we need to add that same name to our list and place it in the *List* sheet for the dropdown to pick it up.

Create the list in the *List* sheet as per Figure 28. Don't forget to include *All* as shown.

	A	B
1	Parent Company List	
2	All	
3	Company ID 0049	
4	Company ID 0034	
5	Company ID 0055	
6	Company ID 0020	
7	Company ID 0005	
8	Company ID 0038	
9	Company ID 0080	
10	Company ID 0090	

Figure 28.

To select your *ActiveX control* (dropdown), go to the *Main* sheet, click on the *DEVELOPER* tab and click **Design Mode** to be allowed to work on the control (if not already clicked). Finally, click once on your dropdown control to select it. See Figure 29.

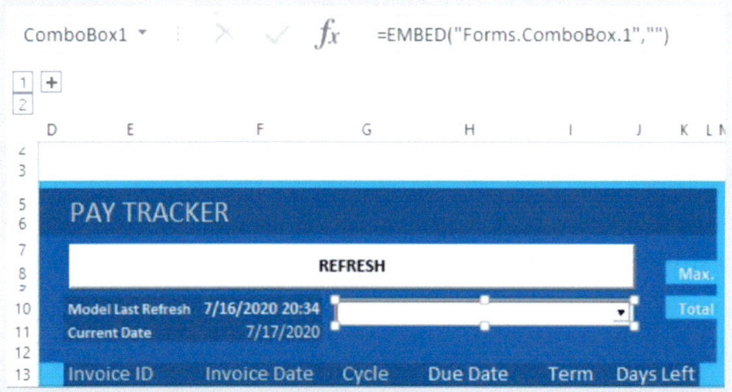

Figure 29.

Note from Figure 29 that the name assigned to the control is ComboBox1. This is important since macros recognize specific controls by their unique name. If you change the name of the control you also need to change its name in the macro (since it's hardcoded).

Next step would be to assign the list we created to the *List* sheet of this control. Do a right click on the dropdown (which is selected) and click on **Properties** as shown in Figure 30.

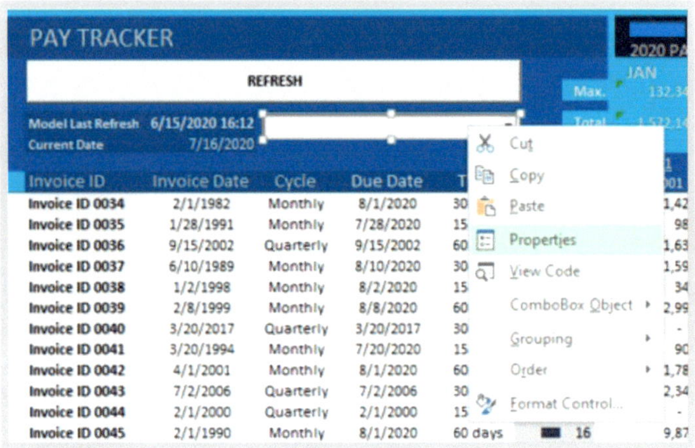

Figure 30.

The window shown in Figure 31 will appear. To assign our list to the control go ahead and type *List!A2:A13* in the **ListFillRange** property as shown in the figure. Close the property window. Go to the *DEVELOPER* tab and deselect **Design Mode**.

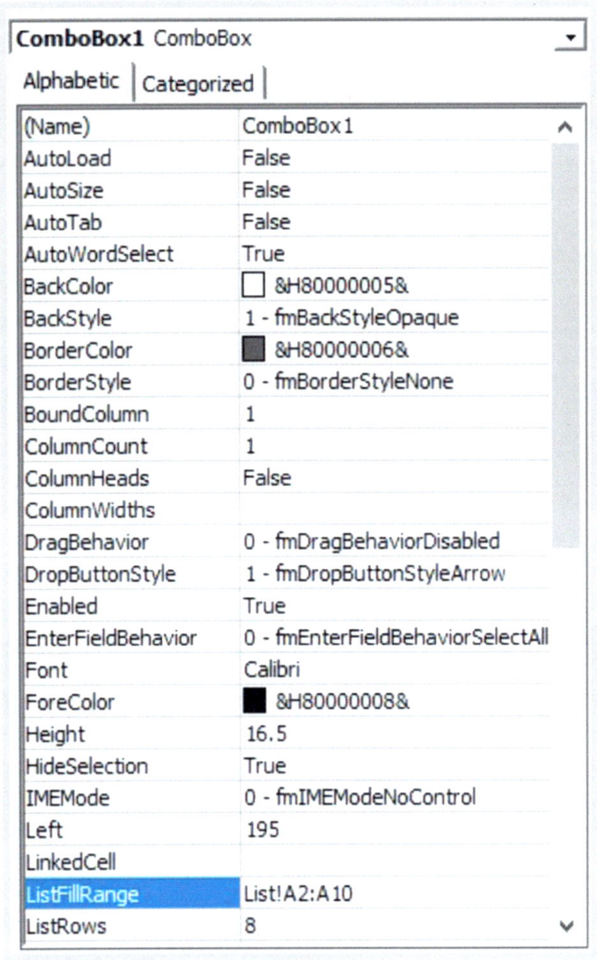

Figure 31.

We're all set to write the code from which this control will feed. Below is the macro we need to write. In this *Private Sub* macro we start by declaring and defining our variables. In this case, variable *x*. Note that variable *x* is a *ComboBox1.value* that translates to: *x* equals the value that is selected in our *ComboBox1*, that is, any value of our list.

After we have completed declaring our variables, we proceed to write instructions. Here's the logic: if x <> (<> means does not equals) "All" (enclosed in quotes) select whatever criteria of *x* is selected in the dropdown (whatever *Company ID* or value) within range A13:A10000. Else, select every value within range A13:A10000.

```
Private Sub ComboBox1_Change()

Dim x As String
x = ComboBox1.Value

If x <> "All" Then
Range(Range("A13:A10000"), Range("A13:A10000").End(xlDown)).Select
Selection.AutoFilter field:=1, Criteria1:=x
Range("F8").Select
Else
Range(Range("A13:A10000"), Range("A13:A10000").End(xlDown)).Select
Selection.AutoFilter field:=1, Operator:=xlFilterValues
Range("F8").Select
End If

End Sub
```

To apply this macro, go to the VBE, double click *Sheet1 (Main)* and copy and paste the code from the source code file into the *Code Window* or type code above. See Figure 32.

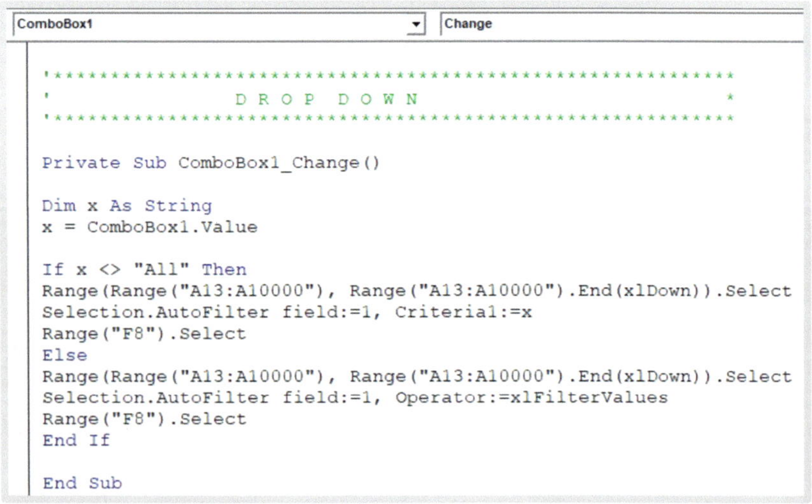
ComboBox1 | Change

```
'*****************************************************************
'                    D R O P   D O W N                           *
'*****************************************************************

Private Sub ComboBox1_Change()

Dim x As String
x = ComboBox1.Value

If x <> "All" Then
Range(Range("A13:A10000"), Range("A13:A10000").End(xlDown)).Select
Selection.AutoFilter field:=1, Criteria1:=x
Range("F8").Select
Else
Range(Range("A13:A10000"), Range("A13:A10000").End(xlDown)).Select
Selection.AutoFilter field:=1, Operator:=xlFilterValues
Range("F8").Select
End If

End Sub
```

Figure 32.

When you click on the dropdown you should see the list/values shown in Figure 33.

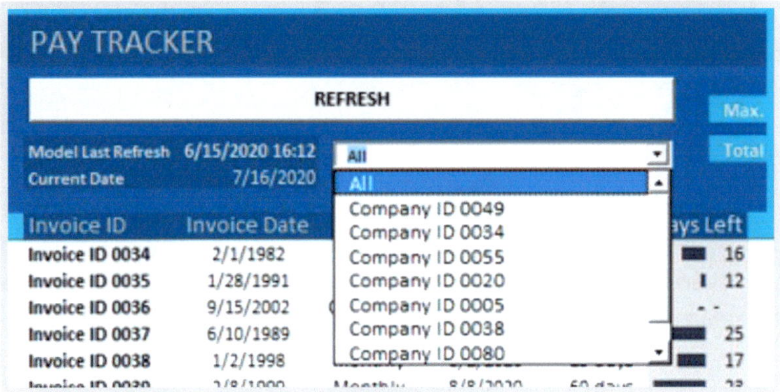

Figure 33.

At this point, your dropdown should be fully functional and able to filter invoices by *Company ID*.

We hardcoded the macro to select range of cells A13:A10000 on the basis that you could have 9,987 invoices in your model. In case you have a higher number of invoices to load into your model, let's say 20,000 invoices, you would need to extend your cell range.

Don't forget to save your work as Excel Macro-Enabled Workbook.

FINAL NOTES

Like any other programmer in this world, you'll encounter issues with your code. My best advice in this case is to overcome frustration by working until a solution is found. We learn to code by solving problems.

Here are some quick notes: if you get an error while running your macro (*Error Break Mode*), go to your VBE, identify highlighted code, click Reset (*Stop button*) and fix the code that was highlighted before running the macro again. If in your *Main* sheet a column is intended to contain dates, then make sure to use *Date* formatting in that specific column.

You've created everything you need to have a functional working model. This model is an open canvas; you can clone macros and functions to add more functionality, or just remove what you don't need. You can create new macros from scratch, modify columns, or add more color to the model. Whatever works for you.

When you have created something that looks reasonably attractive, that makes sense, and is functional, you know you've created something that other people can trust. Every Excel model you create should promote trust and reliability, always.

COMPANION FILES

Please download the companion files from: **https://hollerdata.com/vbdf175093**

Made in the USA
Monee, IL
01 May 2026

49330189R00036